Original title:
Frost-Kissed Paths

Copyright © 2024 Swan Charm
All rights reserved.

Author: Olivia Oja
ISBN HARDBACK: 978-9916-79-759-4
ISBN PAPERBACK: 978-9916-79-760-0
ISBN EBOOK: 978-9916-79-761-7

Under the Shroud of Whispering Winds

Beneath the sky where shadows play,
The whispering winds begin to sway.
Secrets linger in the air,
Tales of love and dreams laid bare.

Leaves dance softly on the ground,
Echoes of past lives profound.
In twilight's glow, the shadows shift,
Time unfolds, a gentle gift.

Stars awaken, twinkling bright,
Guiding hearts through the night.
Silhouettes of memories rise,
Carried forth on silver sighs.

In the hush, we find our peace,
From every burden, a sweet release.
Nature's song, a soothing balm,
Nestled deep, an endless calm.

So let the winds weave through your dreams,
Carrying hope in silver streams.
Under the shroud, our spirits blend,
In whispers soft, love has no end.

Serpentine Shadows in the Snow

Shadows twist beneath the trees,
Winter's breath, a silent tease.
Footsteps ghost through frosted ground,
Nature's whispers, barely found.

Chill embraces all around,
Fleeting shapes in white abound.
Hushed allure of twilight's glow,
Secrets kept in layers of snow.

The Gentle Touch of a Winter's Whisper

Softly falls the silver light,
Whispers dance on quiet night.
Frosty prints on arctic air,
Caress of winter, pure and rare.

Gentle snowflakes twirl and spin,
Wrapping earth in warmth within.
A tender hush in every breath,
The world embraced by chilly death.

Traces of Time in the Glacial Stillness

Frozen moments, time stands still,
Echoes of the mountain thrill.
Layers lie like memories lost,
Each a story, every frost.

Glacial rivers shape the land,
Eroding stones by nature's hand.
Silence speaks where whispers roam,
In the stillness, we find home.

Enchanted Routes Through Glittering Silence

Paths emerge where stillness reigns,
Crystals catch the moonlight's chains.
Magic gleams on every flake,
Mysteries the shadows make.

Step by step through enchanted fields,
Nature's charm, a power yields.
In the silence, find your way,
Guided by the stars' soft play.

Treading Lightly on Icebound Dreams

Whispers of frost beneath my feet,
Echoes of dreams where shadows meet.
Glazed reflections on a crystal tide,
A journey where silence and wonder abide.

Each step a careful, breathless pause,
A moment held without a cause.
The air is crisp with fleeting sighs,
As the world holds its breath and quietly cries.

Beneath the ice, tales pulse with light,
Stories of hope in the heart of night.
I tread softly, as visions gleam,
In the glow of my heart's still dream.

Secrets Beneath the Snowdrift

Beneath the soft white blanket's sigh,
Lies a world echoing, shy and spry.
Secrets buried, waiting for spring,
In the heart of winter, whispers sing.

Each flake that falls hides a tale untold,
Of journeys ventured and memories bold.
Nature's canvas, painted in white,
Shrouds the stories of day and night.

Time moves gently, like a silent stream,
Cradling hopes within every dream.
With each thaw, the past will glow,
Revealing the truths that breathe below.

The Dance of Ice Crystals

In the stillness of a snowy night,
Ice crystals waltz in ethereal light.
Glimmers of silver, sharp and bright,
Sparkle and shimmer, pure delight.

They twirl and spin with grace and flair,
Choreographed by the wintry air.
Each flicker tells a story new,
Of nature's magic, an artist's view.

A ballet composed on frosty ground,
Where silence reigns and peace is found.
In the depths of winter's embrace,
Life dances lightly, tracing its grace.

Winter's Tapestry of Glinting Snow

A tapestry woven with threads of white,
Each flake a star in the quiet night.
Silent whispers dance on the breeze,
Unfolding stories beneath the trees.

Frozen beauty, a moment's sigh,
Painting the earth with a lullaby.
Gentle layers, muffled sound,
Wrap the world in softness profound.

In the hush of winter's serene hold,
Each drift a secret, waiting to be told.
Glimmers of magic entwine and flow,
In the heart of winter, where dreams grow.

Muffled Sounds of the Chilly Wanderer

Whispers of winter fill the night,
Footsteps soft, like fading light.
A breath of frost on every face,
Drifting through this quiet space.

Shadows dance beneath the moon,
Hushed and tranquil, nature's tune.
The chill wraps close, a tender shroud,
In solitude, far from the crowd.

The stars hang low, a glimmering show,
Painted skies where wild winds blow.
Every heartbeat, a rhythmic sound,
In the silence, magic found.

Echoes of tales lost to time,
Carried in frost, pure and sublime.
The chilly wanderer roams with care,
Finding peace in the frostbitten air.

A Tapestry of Ruins in the Snow

Faded walls in blankets white,
Nature's hand, a quiet might.
Crumbled stone and ivy cling,
Stories lost that the cold winds sing.

Amidst the silence, whispers breathe,
History waits, a haunting wreath.
Snowflakes fall on shattered dreams,
Seamless threads, unravelled seams.

Echoes resonate through the years,
Where laughter danced, now only tears.
A tapestry woven, thread by thread,
In the stillness of the dead.

Shadows tremble, ghosts may sway,
In the ruins, memories lay.
With each flake, a tale unwinds,
Of love and loss, the past it finds.

Reflections in the Glacial Mirror

Still waters stare, a frozen gaze,
Beneath the ice, a world ablaze.
Mountains loom, their bold embrace,
Captured softly, a tranquil space.

Captured lights in prisms glow,
Whispers of winds from long ago.
Each ripple speaks of time's embrace,
As nature dons her crystal lace.

In the depths, dark secrets rest,
Layered stories, forever pressed.
The glacial mirror knows no lies,
Reflecting hearts, the dreams that rise.

What lies beneath, a mystery deep,
Found in silence, secrets keep.
Nature's canvas, vast and clear,
In the stillness, all is near.

Guardians of the Snow-Laden Lane

Tall trees stand, their branches bare,
Clad in white, a frosty wear.
Sentinels of the quiet road,
Bearing witness to the snow's load.

Footsteps crunch on powdered trails,
Through the hush, a tale unveils.
Whispers roam where shadows play,
Guarded secrets hold the sway.

Each flake descends like whispered grace,
Carpeting earth in soft embrace.
The lane a path of dreams undone,
Beneath the gaze of winter's sun.

Laden boughs, a fairy's touch,
In their stillness, we feel so much.
The guardians watch, both old and wise,
In their presence, comfort lies.

Celestial Patterns on Frozen Ground

Stars dance above the chilled night,
Their silver glow, a pure delight.
Patterns drawn on frozen seas,
Nature's quilt, a gentle tease.

Moonlight spills on icy trails,
Whispers soft like winter gales.
Footprints fade beneath the frost,
In this world, all time is lost.

Crystals spark on nature's skin,
Silent tales where dreams begin.
Each breath clouds in the cold air,
A moment caught, magic rare.

As dawn breaks, the light returns,
Fires of gold in warmth that burns.
Yet in shadows, echo stills,
The quiet calm, the heart it fills.

Beneath the stars, we find our peace,
In frozen grounds, our doubts release.
Celestial patterns guide our way,
Through night's embrace, until the day.

Whispers of the White Woods

Branches heavy, dressed in white,
The woods breathe softly in the night.
Silence hugs each twisted tree,
Whispers carried by the breeze.

Frosty air, a crystal tune,
Echoes of the gentle moon.
In the stillness, secrets sigh,
Fables woven, low and high.

Shadows stretch as shadows play,
Footsteps mark the path we sway.
Nature's hush in winter's hand,
Guiding us through this quiet land.

Snowflakes fall, a tender grace,
Each a story, a fleeting trace.
Between the pines, a world unfolds,
Magic lost, yet never cold.

In the still, our hearts align,
With the woods that softly shine.
Whispers of the white woods call,
In their embrace, we find our all.

The Path Beneath Diamond Skies

Underneath the diamond skies,
Stars like lanterns, shining eyes.
The way ahead, with frost adorned,
A journey path, freshly formed.

Footsteps crunch on crystal ground,
In the stillness, peace is found.
Each blink of night reveals a tale,
Of dreams that dance in moonlit veil.

Silver clouds drift, soft and slow,
Painting shadows on the snow.
Guided by the light above,
We walk the path, we seek the love.

Voices echo, soft and low,
Carried on the winter's blow.
The night embraces, time stands still,
In this place, our hearts fulfill.

As dawn whispers, stars retreat,
Morning wakes the world, so sweet.
Yet beneath the diamond skies,
The path remains, where spirit flies.

Reflecting on Winter's Shard

Glimmers caught on winter's shard,
Fractals spark, beauty hard.
Ice reflects the sun's embrace,
Each shimmer tells a whispered grace.

In quiet corners, snowflakes drift,
Nature's breath, a gentle gift.
Patterns weave in soft white sheets,
The world transformed beneath our feet.

Chill wraps tight like a lover's vow,
Every moment a frozen now.
We pause to feel the cold perfume,
In this stillness, we find room.

Reflections dance on glassy streams,
Silent echoes of our dreams.
Time slows down, the heart ignites,
In winter's shard, a joy alights.

As dusk descends, the colors fade,
A tapestry of light displayed.
Yet in this quiet, we find our way,
Reflecting on the winter's play.

Spirits Entangled in Winter's Glow

In the chill of twilight's embrace,
Ghostly figures begin to trace.
Whispers dance on frosty air,
A symphony of dreams laid bare.

Snowflakes fall like ancient sighs,
Underneath the pale grey skies.
Each shimmer holds a memory,
Of laughter lost, now set free.

Winds weave tales through barren trees,
Echoing softly, like distant pleas.
The warmth of hearths ignites the night,
In winter's grip, all hearts unite.

Glimmers of hope in shadows play,
In this frozen world, we find our way.
Spirits twirl where silence grows,
Entangled here in winter's glow.

The Solitude of Snow-Covered Trails

Amid the pines, a path unmarked,
Each step whispers, echoing stark.
Solitude wraps its tender arms,
As nature holds her tranquil charms.

Footprints disappear with gentle grace,
Lost in the white, in this sacred space.
The world outside fades into mist,
As silence reigns, and time is kissed.

Branches bow with a heavy load,
While deep in peace, the heart is strode.
In every flake that falls anew,
Lies a promise, a world in view.

Lonely echoes serve as guides,
Through the glades where stillness hides.
A journey carved in icy trails,
The soul finds rest where winter dwells.

Murmurs from the Frosty Expanse

Winds weave softly through the trees,
Carrying secrets with gentle ease.
They chant of places far and wide,
Where frost and freedom both collide.

Across the fields, a quiet song,
Calls to hearts where dreams belong.
Murmurs rise like ghostly smoke,
In this realm where shadows woke.

Crystals glisten on nature's skin,
Wrapped in tales of where we've been.
The frosty expanse sings so clear,
Of winters past, of laughter near.

Breathe in the chill, let worries cease,
In this frozen world, find your peace.
With every murmur that takes flight,
Feel the warmth within the night.

Whirling Flakes and Shadowed Whisperings

Flakes descend like silent dreams,
Spinning softly in silver beams.
Whirling dances in the night,
Shadows flicker, out of sight.

Whispered secrets weave through the dark,
As chilly winds ignite a spark.
In the stillness, stories blend,
Of distant paths that twist and bend.

The moonlight bathes the world in white,
Echoes linger, taking flight.
Through drifts of snow, the echoes play,
Shadowed whispers lead the way.

In this realm of tranquil grace,
Magic swirls in every place.
Whirling flurries, nature's song,
In winter's arms, we all belong.

The Spell of Winter's Canvas

The snowflakes drift like whispers,
Painting the world in white embrace.
Trees wear coats of sparkling crystal,
As silence deepens all around.

Footprints crisscross in the moonlight,
Stories told in soft, cold hush.
Nature holds her breath in wonder,
While stars shimmer in quiet grace.

The night wraps all in quiet magic,
As frost weaves lace on window panes.
Each breath steams in the chilling air,
Creating art in winter's bloom.

In the stillness, time feels frozen,
Moments linger, sweet and rare.
The canvas waits for morning's blush,
To unveil colors bright and bold.

As dawn unfolds with gentle light,
The spell of night begins to fade.
Yet winter's beauty lingers on,
A memory etched in white and blue.

The Dance Beneath the Stars

Underneath the velvet sky,
The universe begins to stir.
Stars twinkle like distant laughter,
Whispers of dreams begin to rise.

Moonlight bathes the earth in silver,
Guiding the dance of shadows' play.
Each movement speaks of ancient stories,
As the night begins to sway.

The breeze carries a song of whispers,
Secrets lost in time's embrace.
Hearts awaken to the rhythm,
Beneath the arch of cosmic grace.

Footsteps meld with nature's heartbeat,
In the silence, souls intertwine.
The dance unfolds in soft, warm glimmers,
Crafting beauty, pure and divine.

As dawn approaches, colors soften,
Painting whispers in the light.
Yet memories of the dance remain,
In the echoes of the night.

The Frosted Horizon Beckons

On the edge of dawn's soft whisper,
The horizon wears a frosted smile.
Each breath a cloud in the stillness,
Calling forth the morning's trial.

The world is cloaked in muted colors,
Where shadows play beneath the sky.
Nature holds her breath in patience,
As the sun begins to rise high.

The air is crisp, a touch of magic,
Each step crunches on frozen ground.
The landscape sparkles, ice and wonder,
In every corner, beauty found.

Horizon glows with hues of amber,
As the night surrenders light.
Tales of winter softly whisper,
In the calm of the fading night.

The frosted world begins to shimmer,
Awaking dreams from icy rest.
With each new dawn, the heart remembers,
The beauty in winter's quest.

A Frosty Ballet of Shadows

In the twilight's gentle closure,
Shadows dance upon the ground.
Frosty breath upon the window,
Hints of magic all around.

Glistening branches sway and shimmer,
Each movement a soft ballet.
Night unfolds her cool enchantment,
Filling silence, night's display.

The moon, a spotlight in the darkness,
Illuminates a world asleep.
While the snowflakes swirl like dancers,
In a spiral, oh so deep.

Gentle whispers grace the stillness,
As the frosty wind takes flight.
Every breath a cloud of wonder,
In the heart of winter's night.

With each step, the stars are twinkling,
Nature's stage, the sky above.
In the ballet of shadows weaving,
Winter sings a song of love.

The Chilling Embrace of Morning Light

The dawn breaks soft and clear,
With whispers in the air.
A chill wraps 'round my soul,
As light begins to dare.

Fingers of the sun reach wide,
Chasing shadows of the night.
Each beam a gentle guide,
Throwing dark into the light.

Birds begin to sing their song,
A symphony so sweet.
The world awakens slowly,
Nature finds its beat.

The frosted grass glimmers bright,
Kissing the earth anew.
A moment held in grace,
Wrapped in morning's hue.

In this embrace, I find my peace,
A promise softly made.
In every breath, I feel released,
From night's cool, deep shade.

Crystal Veils on Winding Ways

Through misty lanes where silence weaves,
Crystal veils dance gently.
Each step reveals a story told,
In echoes pure and plenty.

The path bends like a whispered dream,
Wrapped in nature's lace.
Moments captured in the gleam,
Of time's soft embrace.

Glistening droplets sing their song,
As the world holds its breath.
A tranquility deep and strong,
In every hidden cleft.

Shadows flicker, secrets dwell,
In the heart of this place.
Winding ways cast a spell,
In their tender grace.

With each step I wander forth,
Into a realm so bright.
Nature's hand upon my heart,
Guided by pure light.

Echoes Beneath the Silver Glaze

Beneath the moon's soft silver glow,
Echoes of the night.
Whispers flutter in the breeze,
Bathed in pale, pure light.

Stars hang low, a twinkling cheer,
In the quiet sky.
Songs of lost and found are near,
In the night's soft sigh.

Footsteps on a path so rare,
Every step a tale.
With every heartbeat, I can hear,
Nature's whispered veil.

Reflections dance on waters deep,
Where dreams quietly swirl.
In the calm where secrets seep,
Time begins to unfurl.

These echoes linger in my soul,
Painting memories bright.
In the stillness, I am whole,
Bathed in silver light.

Paths Draped in Glistening Dreams

With morning dew, the paths do gleam,
Wrapped in nature's thread.
Each step I take, a waking dream,
Where thoughts and hopes are bred.

Blossoms sway with gentle grace,
Underneath the sun's warm kiss.
In each corner, I find a space,
Where moments bloom in bliss.

The air is sweet with fragrant cheer,
Inviting hearts to roam.
In this magic, I hold dear,
I find my way back home.

Colors burst in vibrant song,
Nature's brush at play.
Every path where I belong,
Bids me to stay.

In dreams that glisten, I will tread,
With joy upon my face.
For every step, a story spread,
In this enchanted place.

Beneath the Veil of Winter's Caress

Silent whispers cloak the ground,
Softly falling, drifts abound.
Twilight glimmers, frosty breath,
A world of stillness, life in death.

Branches lace with icy thread,
Nature rests upon her bed.
Footsteps echo, muted tone,
Underneath this chill, alone.

Moonlight dances on the snow,
Casting shadows, soft and slow.
Veils of white, a gentle fate,
Holding secrets, whispering late.

Time stands still, the heart will yearn,
For warmth of spring, the seasons turn.
Yet in silence, solace thrums,
In winter's arms, a stillness hums.

Beneath the veil, I find my peace,
In nature's grip, a sweet release.
The world may sleep, yet dreams arise,
Beneath the stars, where silence lies.

Shimmering Silence along a Hidden Way

Where the path winds through the trees,
A whispering hush in the gentle breeze.
Moonlit glimmers on leaves aglow,
Shimmering silence, the night's soft flow.

Hidden treasures in shadows play,
Nature's beauty at close of day.
Footfalls light, as if to tease,
Lost in thought, the heart finds ease.

Branches arch like a lover's embrace,
Welcoming all to this hidden space.
Stars above twinkle with grace,
Guiding souls in this sacred place.

Whispers gather, the night feels bright,
Cloaked in shadows, kissed by light.
Every step reveals a dream,
In shimmering silence, the world's a gleam.

Follow the path where dreams may lie,
Under the gaze of a velvet sky.
In this haven, freedom sings,
Shimmering silence, the peace it brings.

Laid Bare by the Crisp Air's Might

The trees stand tall, their branches bare,
Crisp air lingers, everywhere.
Frosty whispers greet the dawn,
In nature's realm, life's tapestry drawn.

Colors fade, yet beauty remains,
Touched by winter's gentle reins.
Snowflakes twirl like fragile dreams,
Dancing softly in sunlight beams.

Every breath a cloud of white,
Exhaled secrets in morning light.
Nature wakes, yet holds her breath,
Laid bare by the crisp air's depth.

Echoes of laughter from days gone by,
Playful echoes in the night sky.
Memories woven through time's embrace,
Laid bare beneath this wintry grace.

In the stillness, the heart can see,
The beauty found in simplicity.
Craving warmth, the fire ignites,
Laid bare by the crisp air's heights.

Serenity in the Crunch of Frozen Footfalls

Each step forward, a crackling sound,
Frozen footfalls on the ground.
The world is hushed, the air is clear,
In this moment, peace is near.

Snowflakes fall in a gentle hush,
Time feels endless, a sacred rush.
Nature wraps her arms around,
Serenity lost, but now found.

Footprints fade in the morning light,
Stories told of the winter night.
Quiet echoes, the world slows down,
In the crunch, a soft, sweet crown.

Breath of stillness fills the air,
Whispers soft, a lover's care.
Hands held tight, hearts intertwined,
Serenity is what we find.

Each frozen footfall leaves a mark,
A dance of shadows in the dark.
In this beauty, hearts enthrall,
Finding peace in the crunch for all.

Steps on a Whimsical White Canvas

In the hush of soft morning light,
Bright footprints dance with delight.
Whispers of dreams in each trace,
A story unfolds in this space.

Colors swirl in a playful spree,
Each step a note in a melody.
Laughter paints the skies above,
A canvas alive with joy and love.

Through joyful leaps and gentle sways,
Time suspends in blissful plays.
The heart sings where the wild winds roam,
In this wonder, we find our home.

A fleeting moment, captured bright,
We chase the shadows, dance with light.
With each new mark, a story spun,
In the whimsy, we become one.

Secrets Hushed Beneath Icebound Skies

Beneath the chill of a silent night,
Whispers dwell in frosted light.
Secrets lay in shadows deep,
Promises frozen, they guard their keep.

Starry veils hide tales untold,
Of hearts that beat through the cold.
Icicles drip with muted sighs,
Dreams woven in the midnight skies.

Each glance reveals a hidden truth,
A playful echo of lost youth.
In the stillness, we softly cry,
With every breath, the world goes by.

Yet hope glimmers like morning dew,
In the depths, a warmth shines through.
These secrets held, we reveal in time,
In the silence, our souls will rhyme.

The Dance of Leaves in a Frozen Wisp

Leaves flutter down in ghostly grace,
Caught in the breath of winter's space.
They twirl and spin, soft whispers sigh,
In the stillness where moments lie.

Frozen wisps of crystal air,
Each leaf a story, light as prayer.
Glistening trails of gold and brown,
Nature's ballet, the earth's own crown.

The frosty breeze joins the merry play,
As leaves drift on, swept far away.
With each dip and rise, a fleeting glance,
In this silence, we find our dance.

Each spiral twist, a memory caught,
In nature's hold, we lose our thought.
Together we weave through cold and breeze,
In the art of the moment, hearts find ease.

Glacial Echoes of the Heart

In the heart of glaciers, still and wide,
Echoes whisper where dreams abide.
Each crack and shimmer, a tale unspun,
The rhythm of time, softly begun.

Beneath the surface, life does dwell,
Hidden stories in the ice's shell.
Each heartbeat, a pulse in the frozen ground,
In silence, the lost are found.

The chill wraps round, a tender cloak,
In the stillness, we hear the spoke.
Of winds that cry through ages gone,
In glacial whispers, we are drawn.

Tracing steps on this icy art,
In each reflection, we find the heart.
As echoes sing through the frozen night,
Our souls dance softly, bathed in light.

Winter's Gentle Caress

The whispers of the night, so clear,
Blankets of white, the world draws near.
Every branch adorned, a lovely grace,
In the stillness, winter's warm embrace.

Snowflakes dance like dreams in flight,
Transforming earth to glistening white.
As the frost paints all with silent hue,
The heart finds peace in the tranquil view.

Footsteps crunch on frozen ground,
A symphony of nature's sound.
Each breath a cloud, so soft and light,
In winter's realm, all feels just right.

Moonlight shines on the icy stream,
Reflecting night, like a silver dream.
The world feels slow, time stands still,
Wrapped in warmth, against the chill.

In the cozy glow of fireside light,
Stories shared through the winter night.
Hearts come together, spirits soar,
Embracing winter forevermore.

Soft Treads on Crystal Crests

In twilight's hush, all is serene,
Footprints pressed on snow so clean.
A path unfolds beneath the stars,
Magic glistens, near and far.

Gentle whispers tell of dreams,
As moonlight dances on the streams.
Every step, a soft ballet,
Winter's breath carries us away.

Curtains of white in silent gleam,
Nature wraps us in her dream.
Wandering through this frosty sphere,
In every moment, joy is near.

Echoes of laughter fill the air,
Frosty kisses no soul can spare.
Climbing hills with hearts aligned,
In winter's grip, true love we find.

So let us roam these crystal trails,
With gentle steps and whispered tales.
In the stillness, we shall rest,
Winter's gift, forever blessed.

Beneath the Snow's Soft Cloak

Hidden treasures lie below,
Wrapped in winter's purest snow.
Nature sleeps, the world is hush,
Each flake falls with a blessed rush.

A blanket soft, on earth it lays,
Softening sounds in gentle ways.
The sun peeks through, a golden thread,
Kissing the snow while dreams are fed.

Silhouettes of trees stand tall,
Fashioned from the winter's call.
In shadows deep, secrets hide,
Peaceful moments linger wide.

As dusk descends, the world will gleam,
In silver light, a stunning dream.
The night wraps tight, with stars to glow,
A canvas bright, beneath the snow.

So we gather, in warmth and cheer,
Creating memories we hold dear.
With laughter ringing, we embrace,
The magic found in winter's grace.

Frosted Trails of Solitude

In solitude, I tread so light,
On frosted paths of purest white.
A world untouched, where thoughts can flow,
In winter's heart, I come to know.

Each whisper of the chilling air,
Brings solace deep, beyond compare.
With every step, I find my place,
In quiet moments, I embrace.

The trees stand tall, watching me roam,
Guiding my spirit, leading me home.
In winter's breath, I hear the call,
Of nature's voice that binds us all.

Footprints mark where dreams have been,
A journey past the world unseen.
In frosty stillness, the heart will sing,
Of all the joy that winter brings.

And as the sun begins to rise,
Painting the sky with golden sighs.
I stand in awe, forever true,
In frosted trails, I find renew.

Memories Etched in Frozen Air

Whispers of laughter drift and sigh,
Frozen moments, time slips by.
Echoes of joy in a crystal sphere,
Each breath a memory, ever dear.

Frosted windows tell their tale,
Of fleeting warmth, a soft exhale.
Winter's blanket, pure and white,
Shrouds my heart in silent night.

Footprints leading down the lane,
Marking where we danced in rain.
Snowflakes swirling, a soft caress,
In this chill, we find our rest.

Time stands still in the icy breeze,
As shadows stretch among the trees.
With every pulse, the seasons blend,
In frozen air, our spirits mend.

Memories linger, softly spun,
Under the moon, two hearts as one.
Holding tight to every spark,
In this winter's tapestry, we embark.

Luminous Footprints on Cold Terrain

In the hush of winter's grip,
Stars above begin to dip.
Footprints glow upon the ground,
In their silence, peace is found.

The silver moon casts gentle light,
Guiding wanderers through the night.
Crystals glimmer in the dark,
Each step a shimmering mark.

Frozen breath and hearts aglow,
As we move through the soft, white snow.
Luminous paths that softly lead,
Where dreams unfold and spirits feed.

Fires crackle in distant warmth,
Filling souls with sweet comfort.
We chase the echoes of our past,
Through frosted memories, so vast.

With every footstep, stories weave,
In this chilly night, we believe.
Luminous footprints fade away,
Yet the warmth of love will stay.

Glimmers of Dusk's Embrace

The horizon blushes, day withdraws,
As twilight whispers, nature pauses.
Glimmers dance on fading light,
In dusk's embrace, shadows take flight.

Golden hues spill from the sky,
Painting dreams as night draws nigh.
A gentle caress on winter's air,
In the stillness, memories flare.

Stars awaken, a canvas bright,
In the coolness of approaching night.
Flickers of warmth from hearth's embrace,
Illuminate the quiet place.

Moments linger as time unwinds,
Binding hearts, the closeness finds.
In the hushed dusk, our dreams unite,
Wrapped in the magic of fading light.

With every twinkle, stories bloom,
In the velvet dusk, dispelling gloom.
Glimmers of hope weave through the dark,
As we embark on a new spark.

A Breath of Winter's Secrets

Cold winds sweep through the silent trees,
Carrying tales on a crisp, clear breeze.
A breath of winter, crisp and bright,
Unveils the secrets of the night.

Frosted leaves, a shimmering crown,
In the stillness, thoughts unwind.
With every step on powdery ground,
Whispers of magic stir around.

Icicles hang from the eaves so high,
Catching the glow of a silver sky.
Secrets linger in the cool embrace,
Of a world draped in a delicate lace.

Shadows merge with the falling snow,
As the stars begin to show.
Breathless moments softly unfold,
Winter's secrets, a tale retold.

In the quiet, we find the grace,
Of unspoken love and warmth's embrace.
A breath of winter, clear and true,
Whispers the stories known by few.

Timeless Steps on Shimmering Paths

Upon the frozen lake we tread,
Glittering reflections dance ahead.
Silent whispers of the night,
Beneath a moon so soft and bright.

With footsteps light, we roam untold,
Stories in the starry gold.
Each moment cherished, never lost,
In this beauty, we count the cost.

The air is crisp, the world stands still,
A gentle press of winter's thrill.
Nature's canvas draped in white,
Timeless steps in the soft moonlight.

Paths entwined, our hearts align,
With every breath, our souls entwine.
In shimmering silence, dreams are spun,
Forever captured, two become one.

The Allure of Winter's Journey.

A blanket white covers the ground,
In the stillness, magic is found.
On feathered paths where shadows play,
Winter whispers in soft array.

Each tree adorned in sparkling lace,
Time slows down in this wondrous space.
Footfalls echo through the crisp, cool air,
Every heartbeat a tale laid bare.

The journey weaves through frosty pines,
Where silence sings and nature dines.
A moment's peace, a gentle sigh,
With the falling flakes, dreams drift and fly.

In the glow of dusk, the world's aglow,
The allure of winter sets hearts aglow.
Together we wander, hand in hand,
Tracing our stories through the snowy land.

Whispers of the Winter Trail

In twilight's hush, the shadows creep,
Through wooded paths that silence keeps.
Frosty breath on glowing air,
The winter's song is everywhere.

With every footstep, secrets rise,
Underneath the vast, starry skies.
Nature speaks in a language rare,
Whispers of the trail, a timeless prayer.

Icicles hang like crystal chandeliers,
Holding memories of laughter and tears.
Onward we tread, in this twilight trance,
As snowflakes fall, inviting a dance.

The winter's heart beats soft and low,
In each corner, magic seems to grow.
Whispers lead us, gentle and true,
On this trail, I walk with you.

Silent Imprints on Icy Roads

The world is hushed, a blanket white,
With icy roads that shimmer bright.
Every step leaves a tale untold,
In frost-kissed air, we dance bold.

Crystalline paths stretch far and wide,
Whispers of winter as our guide.
Footprints vanish in the falling snow,
A fleeting moment, a soft hello.

Beneath the stars, we wander free,
The night wraps us in tranquility.
Silent imprints, dreams to unfold,
In this winter wonder, we're never cold.

Along the way, the stories blend,
In every turn, we find a friend.
Nature's breath in the chilling night,
On these icy roads, hearts feel light.

Shimmering Alchemy of Cold

In the stillness, frost takes flight,
Casting spells in silver light.
Nature's breath a whispered song,
In this realm, we all belong.

Glistening crystals paint the trees,
Dancing gently with the breeze.
Every flake, a work of art,
Melting softly, warms the heart.

Moonlit nights, a frozen dream,
Reflecting on the icy stream.
Here, the world slows down its race,
A tranquil hush, a loving embrace.

Colors fade as shadows blend,
In this land, the seasons bend.
Magic weaves through every breath,
Embracing life, defying death.

Each moment here feels like a gift,
In winter's charm, our spirits lift.
Shimmering alchemy unfolds,
In the cold, true beauty holds.

Inscribed on Whispering Breezes

Gentle whispers on the air,
Secrets shared without a care.
Leaves that rustle, tales untold,
In their dance, life's warmth enfold.

Echoes of a distant past,
Stories carried, shadows cast.
In the twilight, dreams take flight,
Guided by the stars so bright.

Each soft sigh of nature's breath,
Bridges life and whispers death.
Quiet moments, fleeting grace,
Found in every time and space.

Through the valleys, over hills,
Nature's song, our heart it fills.
Inscribed on breezes that we feel,
A bond with earth that's truly real.

As the sun begins to set,
Memories linger, none forget.
In every sigh, in every sound,
The essence of life can be found.

The Lure of Icy Trails

Beneath the pines, a path unfolds,
Whispers of adventures bold.
Crystals twinkle on the ground,
In this silence, peace is found.

Footprints mark where few have tread,
Winding trails that softly spread.
Each turn brings a sight anew,
Nature's canvas painted blue.

As the cold nips at the nose,
Winter magic deftly flows.
Rivers frozen, still and bright,
Bathe in the soft, glowing light.

Tempting tales within the chill,
Secrets echo, moods will thrill.
With every step, the heart beats strong,
In this beauty, we belong.

The lure of icy trails we heed,
With each adventure, hearts are freed.
Rise and roam, embrace the day,
In winter's grasp, we find our way.

Glistening Pathways of Serenity

Among the trees, the snowflakes fall,
Softly covering nature's call.
In this quiet, time stands still,
Peace descends, a gentle thrill.

Glistening pathways stretch so wide,
Where dreams and life coincide.
Every step, a calming sigh,
Underneath the open sky.

Whispers glide on frosty air,
Nature's breath, a soothing prayer.
Through the chill, our spirits rise,
Together, beneath vast skies.

Stars peek down from heaven's dome,
Illuminating paths we roam.
Each glimmering step we take,
Awakens joy, our hearts awake.

In the landscape draped in white,
We find solace, pure delight.
Glistening pathways lead us home,
In serenity, our hearts will roam.

Song of the Silent Flakes

Whispers of snow in the night,
Gently landing, pure and white.
Each flake dances, soft and slow,
A silent song in the moon's glow.

Blankets of frost on the ground,
A magical hush all around.
Nature slumbers, dreams take flight,
In the embrace of winter's night.

Crystal pendants from the trees,
Caught in shimmering, winter's breeze.
The world transformed, a sight so rare,
Awakening wonder, pure and fair.

Underneath the starlit sky,
Silent echoes as time slips by.
In this serene winter's take,
Hear the beauty that snowflakes make.

With each flake that falls like a tear,
Memories whisper, sweet and clear.
In the quiet, hearts can find,
The gentle peace of winter's kind.

Nightfall's Frosty Hues

Twilight blankets the fading light,
Cold embraces the coming night.
Shadows dance in azure blue,
As winter paints its frosty view.

Stars awaken with silver gleam,
In the silence, the world seems dream.
Bare branches cradle the night's song,
In the chill, where shadows belong.

Whispers flow through the frozen air,
A tender hush beyond compare.
Misty breath on the window pane,
Nature's canvas, quiet, unchained.

Glistening trails of shimmering white,
Crystals gleam in the starry sight.
Every corner, a world anew,
In the hush of nightfall's hues.

Let us wander through this serene,
In the memories soft and keen.
For in the dark's soft embrace,
We find warmth in winter's grace.

The Allure of Icy Horizons

Vast expanses, icy bright,
Horizon dances with pale light.
Endless whispers ride the breeze,
Triumphant over frozen seas.

Mountains stand in regal white,
Guardians wrapped in frosty might.
Their peaks kiss the heavens high,
A stunning view meets the sky.

In the stillness, hearts can roam,
Each step leads us far from home.
Exploring realms of wonder vast,
The call of winter, unsurpassed.

Elegance of a world so cold,
Tales of ice in silence told.
Nature's beauty, crisp and clear,
In every breath, the season near.

Embrace the chill, let spirits soar,
To icy horizons, forevermore.
For in winter's charm, we'll find,
The allure of peace intertwined.

Walking in the Heart of Winter

Footsteps crunch on frosted ground,
A whispering snow is all around.
Beneath the branches, soft and low,
The heart of winter lingers slow.

Layers woven, warm and snug,
A welcome cup, a gentle hug.
Together we find moments bright,
In the cold embrace of night.

The glimmering world, a sight to see,
In winter's heart, we roam carefree.
Every breath a frosty sigh,
Underneath the endless sky.

Time stands still in the moon's embrace,
As laughter dances in this space.
Wrapped in warmth, we pause to dream,
In the chill, life's simple theme.

Walking paths where silence reigns,
In winter's grasp, where beauty remains.
A journey through each frosty breath,
In the heart of winter, we find depth.

Shadows Cast by Quiet Winds

In the stillness, whispers creep,
Among the trees, where secrets sleep.
Shadows dance in the twilight glow,
As the gentle breezes sigh and flow.

Moonlight drapes on the forest floor,
Carrying tales from the night before.
A soft caress, a fleeting kiss,
In quiet moments, we find our bliss.

Leaves rustle with an ancient song,
Echoes of where the heart belongs.
In the hush, the world stands still,
Nature's song, a tender thrill.

Stars awaken in velvet skies,
While darkness swirls in a soft disguise.
Each heartbeat mingles with the breeze,
An unseen bond that brings us ease.

In shadows cast, we find our way,
Through winding paths where spirits play.
With every breath, the night unfolds,
In whispers soft, our story's told.

The Secret Life of Winter's Breath

Beneath the frost, a stillness lies,
Whispers of life beneath cold skies.
In icy breath, secrets entwine,
Winter's heart beats, pure and divine.

Snowflakes flurry, each unique dance,
Caught in moments of fleeting chance.
The chill wraps tight, a soft embrace,
In this quiet, we find our place.

Bare branches stretch in graceful arcs,
Reaching for warmth, igniting sparks.
In frozen dreams, the world awaits,
For spring's return to open gates.

The crackling fire sings of cheer,
Bringing light to what we hold dear.
In every drift and every flake,
Silent promises that we make.

The hush of night, a blanket wide,
While stars reflect in the snow's glide.
In winter's breath, we trust and tread,
In its tender grasp, hope is fed.

Wonders Wrapped in Frozen Light

Crystal formations, nature's art,
Framing the world, a frozen heart.
Glistening jewels in morning's hue,
Wonders wrapped in a sparkling view.

Each breath turns to mist, swirling low,
As sunlight kisses the falling snow.
A landscape dressed in white delight,
Awakens dreams in morning's light.

Trees draped in lace, a magical sight,
Shimmer and sway as day turns bright.
The air is crisp, filled with delight,
In this serene, enchanted night.

Chasing shadows, the day unfolds,
Within the frost, a tale retold.
Nature cradles her quiet song,
In frozen light, where we belong.

Wonders whisper through winter skies,
Echoing softly as time flies.
In every spark, a promise gleams,
Within the cold, we weave our dreams.

The Sigh of Frosty Nights

When evening falls, a hush descends,
A tranquil world where silence blends.
Frost kisses the earth, a gentle sigh,
As stars twinkle like silver high.

The moon floats soft, a guiding light,
Illuminating dreams of the night.
In the stillness, hearts find their pace,
Wrapped in shadows, we find our space.

Wind whispers secrets through the trees,
Swaying softly with a tender breeze.
Every breath carries a frosty song,
In winter's embrace, where we belong.

Blankets of white cover all that's near,
While echoes of laughter linger here.
Frosted lamps in the windows glow,
Painting the night in a soft warm flow.

As night deepens, wonders appear,
In the sigh of frost, all feels clear.
Through quiet moments, we seek the light,
In the solace of frosty nights.

Silent Glades of Icy Wonder

In glades of ice, stillness reigns,
Whispers of frost in silver chains.
Beneath the snow, the secrets sleep,
Silent dreams in shadows creep.

Glistening branches, a crystal show,
Moonlit trails where cold winds blow.
Hearts entwined in winter's fold,
Eternal stories quietly told.

The air is sharp, each breath a gem,
Nature's breath, a soft diadem.
In the silence, we find our way,
In icy glades, we choose to stay.

A world transformed beneath the light,
Each flake a star, so pure and bright.
In tranquil beauty, we wander free,
In silent glades, just you and me.

Wrapped in dreams, we dare to roam,
In winter's arms, we find our home.
Through frozen whispers, hand in hand,
In icy wonder, we take our stand.

Journey Through the Frostbitten Forest

Through frostbitten trees, we make our way,
Where shadows dance and cold winds play.
Each step a crunch on icy ground,
In nature's hush, a peace profound.

The trail winds deep where silence lies,
A world of wonder under grey skies.
Each branch adorned with frosted lace,
In this enchanted, timeless space.

The air is crisp, a sparkling chill,
As whispers of magic our senses fill.
Following paths where creatures glide,
In the forest's heart, we coincide.

The frozen brook sings soft and low,
In the chill of dusk, we feel the glow.
Every breath a testament to grace,
In frostbitten woods, we find our place.

With every turn, the mystery grows,
In the heart of the forest, adventure flows.
A journey through time, as we contend,
In nature's embrace, we find a friend.

Embracing the Bitter Enchantment

In bitter cold, where magic lies,
We sip the frost from midnight skies.
Embraced by shadows, deep and long,
In this winter's song, we belong.

The frozen air, a breath of art,
Each flake a whisper, a frozen heart.
In enchanted realms, our spirits soar,
Through icy halls, forevermore.

Alone with echoes of ancient lore,
In a world where enchantment pours.
The stars above, a frozen dream,
In the night's embrace, we softly gleam.

Through every chill, a warmth we find,
In the bitter sweet, our hearts aligned.
With every shiver, we learn to feel,
In this enchanted chill, time will heal.

A journey shared with the moonlit night,
In bitter beauty, we take flight.
Hand in hand, through frost and fire,
In this embrace, our hearts aspire.

The Chill of Enchanted Trails

On enchanted trails, the chill unfolds,
Nature's secrets, shrouded in gold.
With every breath, the magic flows,
Deep in the woods where wonder grows.

The frost will paint the world anew,
A canvas bright, a tranquil view.
Through arching boughs and twinkling light,
In the crisp air, our souls take flight.

The silence holds a story's weight,
In every corner, a twist of fate.
With wonder coursing through our veins,
We wander where the mystery reigns.

With each step forward, time stands still,
In the chill of night, we feel the thrill.
To dance with shadows, wild and free,
On enchanted trails, just you and me.

We leave our footprints in the snow,
In the forest's heart, our spirits grow.
Through every chill, this journey binds,
In the enchanted trails, our love unwinds.

Hushed Footsteps on Hallowed Ground

Silence wraps the ancient trees,
Footsteps linger on the breeze.
Shadows dance in twilight's glow,
Time stands still, the world moves slow.

Echoes of the past resound,
Memories on hallowed ground.
Each step whispers stories old,
Secrets in the silence told.

Moonlight bathes the sacred space,
Softly touching every place.
In this realm of quiet sighs,
Hushed footsteps hold the night's replies.

Stars above begin to gleam,
Guiding us like a dream.
Every path is carved in fate,
As we wander, contemplate.

Here we find our souls entwined,
In the stillness, peace we find.
Hushed footsteps in the dark,
Light the way, ignite the spark.

The Silver Thread of a Snowy Journey

Winding roads under a quilt,
Snowflakes dance, a world rebuilt.
Each flake tells a tale anew,
In the stillness, whispers brew.

The silver thread that weaves and sways,
Guiding hearts through winter's maze.
Footprints mark the soft, white grass,
Tracing paths as moments pass.

Horizon glows in twilight's hand,
Painting dreams across the land.
In the chill, warmth starts to rise,
Hope ignites as daylight dies.

Branches laden, heavy with snow,
Nature's beauty, soft and slow.
Every corner wrapped in white,
A canvas blank, pure and bright.

Through this journey, spirits blend,
A snowy path, without an end.
The silver thread, our hearts align,
In this moment, yours and mine.

Frosty Veins of the Earth's Lullaby

Whispers in the morning chill,
Nature breathes, the world stands still.
Frosty veins pulse soft and low,
Underneath the wintry glow.

Every blade of grass adorned,
With glistening jewels, freshly born.
As the sun begins to rise,
A lullaby that never dies.

Crimson dawn paints the sky bright,
Touching frost with gentle light.
Nature's heartbeat, calm and pure,
Frosty veins, a timeless cure.

In stillness, secrets gently weave,
A soft embrace, we believe.
Songs of earth sing sweetly clear,
In this moment, draw us near.

Underneath the frost and snow,
Life's rhythms pulse, soft and slow.
Cradled in the earth's own song,
In these veins, we all belong.

Wandering Through the Whispering White

In a world of softest white,
Wandering in the pale moonlight.
Every step a gentle sigh,
Listening close to the night sky.

Echoes of the trees around,
Whisper secrets, quiet sound.
The snowflakes kiss the frozen ground,
In their dance, magic is found.

Winding paths where silence reigns,
Through the fields, where peace remains.
Every moment feels so bright,
As we drift through this pure night.

Wrapped in warmth of winter's glow,
Bearing tales only snow can show.
Each flake tells its tale in flight,
As we wander, hearts unite.

In the hush, we find the grace,
Lost in time, in this place.
Whispering white, a calming sea,
In this journey, you and me.

Muffled Steps on Silvery Roads

The winter hush, it blankets all,
Soft whispers underfoot do call.
Each step a ghost, a fleeting trace,
On silvery roads, we find our pace.

The trees stand tall, with arms out wide,
Snowflakes dance, a gentle glide.
Beneath the sky, a canvas grey,
Muffled steps lead me on my way.

A quiet charm in nature's breath,
Reminds us of the warmth of health.
With every crunch, a story spun,
In the embrace of winter's fun.

The world feels small, so close, so dear,
In frosted air, I shed my fear.
Each silent pause, a moment's grace,
Muffled steps give me my place.

A journey shared in silent trust,
With every flake that turns to dust.
On silvery roads, our hearts align,
In winter's hold, our souls entwine.

The Artistry of Frosted Foliage

Nature's brush, with icy strokes,
Adorns the leaves in crystal cloaks.
Each blade of grass, a jeweled sight,
In morning's glow, pure and bright.

Frosted patterns, intricate lace,
On every branch, a delicate grace.
The artistry in silence speaks,
Among the trees, where stillness peaks.

In hues of white, a masterpiece,
The world transformed, a sweet release.
A fleeting moment, life's brief pause,
In frozen time, the heart withdraws.

The breath of winter, crisp and clear,
Paints memories held so dear.
Under the spell of fragile sights,
Nature whispers through the nights.

Look closely now, the art unfolds,
In silence, magic softly molds.
Through frosted foliage, life remains,
A canvas kissed by winter's reins.

Traces of Winter's Solitude

In still of snow, the world feels vast,
Footprints linger, memories cast.
A trail of whispers, soft and light,
In winter's grasp, we find our sight.

The trees embrace the heavy air,
They hold the secrets, soft and rare.
Each branch a tale of nights alone,
In solitude, the heart has grown.

Frozen rivers mirror the sky,
Reflecting dreams that gently sigh.
In quiet corners, shadows play,
As winter wraps the world in gray.

The hush brings forth a soothing peace,
In solitude, the mind's release.
Traces linger from days gone by,
In winter's chill, we learn to fly.

Embrace the cold, let silence reign,
For in its depths, we shed our pain.
Traces of winter, pure and bright,
Guide us gently through the night.

The Call of Glacial Waters

A whisper flows from depths below,
Glacial waters, pure as snow.
They sing a tune of ancient times,
In liquid verse, nature climbs.

The rivers glint, a shining thread,
Through valleys deep, where dreams are fed.
Currents dance in rhythmic play,
Calling forth the light of day.

Each ripple tells a story clear,
Of icy realms that draw us near.
The call of water, wild and free,
Invites our hearts to seek the sea.

Reflections spark with hues of blue,
As sunlit whispers come to view.
In tranquil streams, we find our rest,
The essence of life, nature's quest.

From glacial heights to ocean's swell,
The call of waters casts its spell.
In flowing grace, we learn to roam,
In every drop, we find our home.

By the Light of Glistening Havens

In the dawn's embrace, soft warmth breaks,
Waves of gold dance on bright lakes.
Glistening havens in morning's glow,
Whispers of dreams that gently flow.

Trees adorned with jeweled frost,
Echoes of melodies never lost.
Nature sings in vibrant hues,
In this beauty, we quietly muse.

The air is sweet with fragrant blooms,
Laughter rises in joyful rooms.
Children play in endless light,
As day fades softly into night.

Glowing lanterns now take flight,
Guiding us through the tender night.
Hand in hand, with hearts aglow,
By the light of havens, we shall go.

In every step, the promise stays,
Of love and hope in myriad ways.
Together, we'll chase shadows away,
By the light of glistening day.

Edges of Deep Silence in Winter's Fold

White blankets drape on sleeping ground,
Nature's hush, a soothing sound.
Frost-kissed whispers touch the air,
A tranquil scene, so pure, so rare.

Branches bow with icy grace,
Each echo finds a silent place.
Footsteps soft on powdered lane,
Imprints fading with the grain.

A world transformed, so still, so bright,
In winter's fold, we find our light.
Breathe in deep, let worries cease,
In this silence, we find peace.

Snowflakes fall like wishes made,
On every rooftop, in every glade.
Adorned in white, the night begins,
As dreams awaken, the heart spins.

Holding close this frozen time,
In the deep silence, we will climb.
Edges of winter, softly unfold,
A magic woven, forever bold.

The Silent Chronicle of Winter Wanderings

Beneath the stars, the quiet road,
Footsteps trace a hidden code.
Whispers of stories in the snow,
Footprints lead where the cold winds blow.

Each flake a tale from ages past,
In the frosty night, shadows cast.
The icy breath of winter's breeze,
Tales of wanderers through the trees.

A lantern's glow, a beacon bright,
Guiding dreams in the still of night.
With every turn, a memory found,
In the silent chronicle abound.

Frozen lakes reflect the time,
Nature's rhythm, a gentle rhyme.
In the hush, the heart expands,
Holding close the winter's strands.

Wander forth, let spirits soar,
In adventures that we can't ignore.
The silent tale of winter's way,
Guides us gently to the day.

Encounters in the Realm of Snowlight

In the realm where moonlight glows,
Magic sparkles as winter flows.
Snowlight dances on every ridge,
Bridges made of dreams and age.

Figures emerge from the swirling mist,
With joyful tales and hearts like fists.
Laughter echoes in the deep night,
Encounters born in the snowlight's flight.

Every face tells a story grand,
In the sparkle of this enchanted land.
Moments woven like threads so fine,
Connections formed, a warm design.

Gentle winds carry voices near,
As the world spins, we've nothing to fear.
In this luminous realm, we find,
A dance of souls, beautifully blind.

Together we cherish these precious hours,
Lost in wonder, like blooming flowers.
In the realm of snowlight's embrace,
We find our home, our destined place.

Winter's Whispered Embrace

In silent nights, the stars do gleam,
Snowflakes dance in a gentle dream.
Softly falls the icy lace,
Nature's breath, a fleeting grace.

Frosted trees stand tall and bright,
Blanketing the world in white.
Whispers chill the crisp, fresh air,
Winter's magic everywhere.

Beneath the skies of deepened blue,
The moonlight casts a silver hue.
Footprints trace the paths we roam,
In winter's heart, we find our home.

A crackling fire, warmth we seek,
With every laugh, the joy we speak.
Wrapped in blankets, stories flow,
In winter's embrace, love will grow.

As seasons shift, the blooms will rise,
Yet in the frost, our souls comprise.
In every flake, a tale we share,
Winter's whispers fill the air.

Crystal Dreams Beneath the Moon

Beneath the moon, the world aglow,
A crystal dream, where secrets flow.
Stars like diamonds grace the night,
Whispers of magic, shining bright.

Frozen rivers gleam like glass,
Time slows down, as moments pass.
In this realm of silver light,
Hearts take flight in sheer delight.

The trees adorned in icy veils,
Capture stories in their trails.
Nature's beauty, pure and rare,
In crystal forms, beyond compare.

With every breath, the cold is near,
Yet warmth awakens in the cheer.
Together, dreams are spun so fine,
As we embrace this night divine.

From every flake, a tale unfolds,
In whispered secrets, life beholds.
Beneath the moon, we find our way,
In crystal dreams, forever stay.

Frozen Footprints in Twilight

In twilight's glow, the silence speaks,
Frozen footprints mark the peaks.
Each step a memory we trace,
As shadows dance, we find our place.

Whispers linger in the frost,
In every breath, we count the cost.
Yet through the chill, our spirits rise,
In winter's breath, we find our ties.

The fading light, a gentle sigh,
As stars awaken in the sky.
Nature's canvas, bold and bright,
Holds our dreams in soft twilight.

A fleeting moment, time stands still,
In frozen paths, we feel the thrill.
As echoes of the past unite,
We walk together, hearts alight.

With every flake, a story told,
In winter's arms, we are consoled.
Through frozen footprints, love will grow,
In twilight's charm, we come to know.

Glacial Traverses

Through frozen realms, our spirits soar,
On glacial paths, forevermore.
With every step, the world reveals,
A beauty deep that time conceals.

Mountains rise with snow-capped crowns,
Echoes whisper through the towns.
In icy winds, our laughter flows,
As nature's glow in stillness grows.

Rivers carve through ancient stone,
A testament to all we've known.
With every twist, the journey bends,
On glacial traverses, time transcends.

Stars above in velvet skies,
Guide us through the coldest highs.
In winter's grasp, we find our flame,
A bond unbroken, strong, and tame.

As morning breaks, the sun will rise,
Life returns with warm surprise.
Yet in our hearts, we'll always keep,
The glacial paths where dreams run deep.

Veins of Ice and Air

In the stillness, breath is caught,
Veins of ice, the world is naught.
Frost lingers on the silent trees,
Whispers float upon the freeze.

Brittle branches, glistening bright,
Encased in silver, pure delight.
Nature sleeps, draped in white,
A hushed embrace of frozen night.

Every step, a crunching sound,
In this realm where chill is crowned.
The air is crisp, each moment clear,
Veins of ice, where dreams appear.

Footprints trace a fleeting path,
Chasing echoes, nature's laugh.
Underneath the frozen sheen,
Life awaits, though seldom seen.

Frigid whispers, tales untold,
In the air, the silence bold.
Veins of ice in twilight's glow,
A magic dance, soft and slow.

The Silver Lace of Frost

Morning breaks with gentle grace,
The silver lace begins to trace.
Patterns woven, fine and bright,
Embroidered dreams in morning light.

Upon the grass, a shimmering sheet,
Each blade adorned, a frosty treat.
Nature's jewels, a delicate show,
In fleeting moments, a tranquil glow.

Whispers ride on the chilly air,
The silver lace, a silent prayer.
Woven magic, soft and fine,
In whispers, the world aligns.

Eager sun begins to rise,
Casting warmth through frosted skies.
A dance of light, as shadows play,
The silver lace, then fades away.

The day unfolds, yet echoes stay,
Of silver threads in morning's sway.
An ode to frost, a fleeting song,
In nature's heart, where we belong.

Glimmers of Glassy Mornings

Glimmers shine on dawn's embrace,
A glassy world, a peaceful space.
Each crystal glint, a wondrous sight,
Awakens dreams in soft daylight.

Reflections dance on surfaces bright,
Mirrors of magic, pure delight.
In every corner, secrets spun,
Glimmers sparkling, one by one.

The air is crisp, yet warm and new,
In this moment, all feels true.
Nature's canvas, painted clear,
Glimmers whisper, drawing near.

Footsteps echo on the glass,
Time stands still, in shadows pass.
A fleeting touch, a breath of air,
Glimmers captured, a perfect pair.

In the heart where stillness lives,
Glimmers offer what nature gives.
A world reborn, pure and bright,
Glassy mornings, a gentle light.

Ethereal Frosts on Silent Grasses

Ethereal frosts, a quiet veil,
On silent grasses, soft and pale.
Each blade like glass, a frozen sigh,
Whispers of winter, drifting by.

Morning dew meets frost's embrace,
Nature's art in delicate lace.
A tapestry of white and green,
In whispers, the world is serene.

The sun begins to rise and glow,
Painting warmth on fields below.
Yet still the frosts cling tenderly,
To every blade, a memory.

Footprints trace a gentle line,
In ethereal beauty, we entwine.
Nature's breath, a soft refrain,
On silent grasses, hope remains.

Ethereal moments, fleeting fast,
Hold the memory of the past.
In every frost, a story told,
On silent grasses, dreams unfold.

Treading Lightly on an Icy Canvas

A whispering breeze cools the air,
Footsteps crunch like glass laid bare.
Nature's breath paints hues so bright,
On this canvas of frozen white.

Each step a dance, each glance a thrill,
Waves of silence, a quiet chill.
Frosted edges, a world held tight,
In this wonderland, pure delight.

Twinkling stars in the night sky,
Reflecting dreams as they drift by.
The moon bathes the landscape in grace,
An ethereal glow, a sacred space.

Branches glisten with a crystal charm,
Nature's embrace, a soothing balm.
In this beauty, worries seem small,
Treading lightly, caring for all.

Each moment savored, a fleeting scene,
In this icy dream, so serene.
The heartbeat of winter, soft and slow,
On this canvas, life's essence flows.

The Luminescence of Narnia's Path

Through the trees, a path does gleam,
A tapestry woven from dreams.
Footprints fresh upon the snow,
Whispers of magic that softly glow.

With each turn, the world reveals,
Secrets held in icy seals.
The air, alive with an ancient song,
Guides the way where hearts belong.

Beneath the trees, a light does dance,
In the stillness, a spellbound trance.
Narnia waits with its wondrous sight,
Bathed in the warmth of the moon's light.

Crystals sparkle like gems so rare,
Painting stories in the frosty air.
A flicker of hope in every breath,
Renewing life where dreams have left.

A journey unfolds with every stride,
With shadows and light, side by side.
In this realm, where magic weaves,
The path leads to what the heart believes.

Whispering Pines Beneath Frozen Stars

Amidst the pines, the silence reigns,
A symphony of icy plains.
Stars shimmer like diamonds bright,
Guiding souls through the winter night.

Beneath the canopy, shadows play,
As moonlight dances on the way.
Frosty branches, a delicate lace,
In this quiet, a sacred space.

Whispers of wind carry stories old,
Of journeys undertaken, brave and bold.
Through the night, a gentle call,
Inviting the dreamers, one and all.

In frozen realms where spirits fly,
Each breath is a promise, a sigh.
The stars remind us, we are not lost,
In this quiet world, we bear the cost.

So walk with me 'neath the frozen glow,
Where nature's secrets ebb and flow.
In the hush of the night, we find our way,
With whispering pines, at the end of day.

A Bridge of Ice Between Dawn and Dusk

A bridge of ice, a shimmering span,
Linking the stories of nature's plan.
In the glow of dawn, colors collide,
As daybreak whispers secrets inside.

The sun's first rays kiss the icy hue,
Painting the path with a vibrant view.
As shadows stretch and dance with grace,
Time holds still in this sacred space.

With each heartbeat, the world unfolds,
Tales of wonder waiting to be told.
A bridge of dreams where the heart feels free,
Connecting the earth and the vast sea.

In the twilight glow, the sky ignites,
Casting spells in the fading lights.
As dusk embraces the day's sweet breath,
We traverse the bridge, escaping death.

So let us wander, hand in hand,
Across this bridge, through icy land.
Where dawn meets dusk in a timeless dance,
In this frozen world, we find our chance.

Icebound Memories

Frozen whispers in the air,
Carried secrets everywhere.
Once warm smiles now cold as stone,
Echoes of a time unknown.

Shadows dance on icy walls,
Listening to the silence calls.
Each breath taken, a ghostly sigh,
In the stillness, memories lie.

Blankets thick of soft white snow,
Hiding tales of long ago.
Time stands still, as moments freeze,
Longing drifts on winter's breeze.

Frosted branches, trees embrace,
Nature holds a timeless grace.
In the chill, I find a spark,
A flicker light within the dark.

Yet memories still make me weep,
In shadows where the silence keeps.
Icebound dreams and whispers fade,
In the heart where warmth is laid.

Cold Echoes of Forgotten Steps

Footprints lost in drifts of white,
Silent paths under moonlight.
Each step echoes a silent tale,
Of laughter gone, of dreams frail.

Winter winds whisper about,
Speaking softly, filled with doubt.
Memories linger, emotions fray,
In the cold, they quietly stay.

Chill wraps 'round like a shroud,
A distant song, once bold and loud.
Now just echoes, fading fast,
Ghosts of steps that cannot last.

Bare branches scratch the winter sky,
A reminder of the days gone by.
In the frost, the stories creep,
Chilling truths that make us weep.

Yet in this quiet, I still stand,
Holding tight to nature's hand.
Even cold can bring us near,
To memories we hold dear.

The Glisten of Morning Chill

Morning breaks with a gentle glow,
Frozen dew on blades of low.
Each drop glistens, pure and bright,
A fleeting moment, a soft light.

Sunrise kisses icy ground,
In its warmth, new life is found.
Chill retreats to shadows near,
While nature stirs, again we cheer.

Whispers of a brand new day,
In the chill, hopes find their way.
Through the fog, a path is made,
In the light, our dreams invade.

Crystals dance on winter's breath,
A sparkle placed where life felt depth.
In the morning's tender thrill,
Lies a promise of warmth to fill.

So greet the dawn with open heart,
From the cold, we will not part.
In every glisten, a story speaks,
Of warming hope in winter's peaks.

Chilling Secrets in Stillness

In the stillness, secrets hide,
Frozen whispers coincide.
Winter's grasp holds tightly fast,
In the silence, shadows cast.

Each flake that falls, a tale untold,
Stories of the brave and bold.
Amidst the beauty, lies the pain,
Hidden truths from love's disdain.

Branches sway in coldest breath,
Each creak and crack hints at death.
Yet in the calm, the world will know,
Secrets buried beneath the snow.

Silhouettes in the moon's embrace,
Stillness wears a solemn face.
Chilling secrets hover near,
Waiting for someone to hear.

But in stillness, hope prevails,
Breaking free from winter's scales.
Each secret shared, no longer thrall,
In the quiet, we stand tall.

A Walk Through the Crystal Realm

Beneath the arch of gleaming skies,
A world of light in sharp surprise,
Crystal paths that softly gleam,
In each step, a whispered dream.

Through icy woods, the shadows play,
Where echoes of the past hold sway,
Glistening branches, silver lace,
Invite the heart to slow its pace.

Footprints trace a path unknown,
Through frosted air, the chill is grown,
A dance of nature, pure and grand,
In the crystal realm, we take our stand.

The sun, a gem on winter's crown,
A glimmering jewel in twilight's gown,
With every breath, the magic swells,
In silent woods where beauty dwells.

As twilight deepens, colors blend,
A fusion of worlds, where visions bend,
In the crystal realm where spirits flow,
We find the peace we yearn to know.

Solstice Reflections

In the hush of longest night,
Stars awaken, shimmering bright,
Fires crackle, tales unwind,
Hope reborn, and hearts aligned.

Shadows stretch as daylight fades,
Silent prayers in nature's shades,
Moonlit dreams on winter's breath,
Reflections filled with life and death.

Candles glow in windows wide,
Warming souls who bide inside,
A time for rest, a time to heal,
In solstice magic, we feel real.

With every flicker, memories rise,
Of laughter shared and whispered sighs,
In the darkness, love's gentle spark,
Guides us through the cold and dark.

As dawn breaks, new light will stream,
We step into the brightened dream,
Solstice hope, a guiding star,
Together, we'll venture far.

The Aria of Winter Walks

In the crisp air, a song so clear,
Notes of winter, sweet and dear,
Each step a rhythm in perfect time,
With nature's pulse, a gentle rhyme.

The trees sway softly, branches bow,
An aria sung by the silent bough,
Whispers of snow on the wind's embrace,
In every flake, a frosty grace.

Footsteps crunch on fallen leaves,
Where the breath of winter weaves,
A tapestry of white and gray,
Guiding the heart on its way.

With every corner, a new surprise,
Hidden beauty that never lies,
Sunlight dances on frozen streams,
In the aria of winter dreams.

So let us wander, hand in hand,
Through winter's grasp, a wonderland,
For in each moment, life's tune plays,
In the melody of snow-kissed days.

Veils of Ice in the Fading Light

As daylight wanes, shadows creep,
Veils of ice, secrets to keep,
Glimmers fade on the frosty ground,
In silence, beauty can be found.

The sun dips low, a fiery thread,
Painting the sky with hues of red,
Ice crystals catch the dying glow,
A whisper of warmth in the chill below.

Branches draped in winter's lace,
A fragile art, a timeless grace,
Each moment holds a fleeting sight,
In veils of ice, the world ignites.

With every breath, the cold bites deep,
Yet in this hush, the heart can leap,
For in the dusk, all fears take flight,
Under veils of ice in fading light.

In twilight's grasp, we find our peace,
As nature's symphony finds release,
Emerge from shadows, embrace the night,
In the magic of veils, we take delight.

Journey Through the Shimmering Chill

A path unfurls beneath the pale,
Where whispers dance with frosty air.
Our footsteps crunch on sparkled trails,
In winter's grasp, we walk with care.

The trees, adorned in icy lace,
Stand guard above the winding way.
Each breath, a cloud, a fleeting trace,
Of moments seized before they fray.

The sun dips low, a golden gem,
Casting shadows long and wide.
We journey forth, no time to stem,
The vibrant pulse that we can't hide.

In stillness, life begins to hum,
The echoes of a soft refrain.
A melody that calls us home,
Through shimmering chill, our hearts remain.

As frost-kissed stars light up the night,
We find a warmth within the cold.
In every step, in pure delight,
A journey's tale begins to unfold.

The Soft Caress of Icebound Moments

A fragile touch, the world stands still,
As time drips slowly without haste.
Each glimmering flake a dream to fill,
Our souls entwined, the sweetest taste.

Whispers brush against the night,
With echoes soft as twilight falls.
We gather warmth from fading light,
In icebound moments, love recalls.

The trees, like sentinels, so grand,
Embrace the beauty of their plight.
In silence, hand in hand we stand,
Our hearts aglow with pure delight.

The world may freeze, the winds may chill,
Yet here we find a sheltered space.
In soft caress, we feel the thrill,
Of time where memories embrace.

As snowflakes weave their quiet tale,
We carve our path, a love's design.
In every heartbeat, dreams prevail,
In icebound moments, so divine.

Veils of White on Worn Out Trails

Beneath the weight of winter's sigh,
A tapestry of white unfurls.
We've walked this path, yet still we try,
To trace the lines of hidden pearls.

The footprints of the days gone by,
Are softened now, like whispered dreams.
With every step, we question why,
The past still flows in silver streams.

As shadows stretch, the twilight glows,
A gentle hush wraps round the trees.
The memories linger, ebb and flow,
In veils of white, our hearts appease.

Along these trails, we've loved and lost,
Yet here we carry on our way.
With every step, we count the cost,
And marvel at what dreams convey.

Through veils of white, our spirits soar,
In nature's grasp, we find the grace.
While worn out trails recall before,
New journeys wait, a warm embrace.

Twinkling Crystals Beneath Moonlight

In velvet night, the world aglow,
With twinkling crystals, soft and bright.
Each diamond twirl, a gentle show,
That dances silently in the light.

The moonbeams weave a silver lace,
Upon the earth, a sacred bond.
Reflecting dreams in time and space,
Where hearts unite and fears abscond.

With every sigh, the echoes play,
An ancient tune, a lover's song.
In quiet moments, night to sway,
We find our place, where we belong.

The chill ignites a fiery spark,
As laughter mingles with the cold.
In twinkling realms where shadows mark,
Our stories blend, like dreams retold.

Beneath the sky, so vast and deep,
We trace the path of starlit dreams.
In twinkling crystals, secrets keep,
While moonlight holds our whispered themes.

Celestial Gauntlet of Ice

Beneath the starlit, frosty veil,
The moon hangs, cold and pale,
Each flake a whisper, silent flight,
Through the vast and icy night.

A frozen breath paints the sky,
As shadows dance and gently sigh,
Crystals shimmer, sharp and clear,
In this realm where dreams appear.

Glistening paths of silver light,
Guide the wanderers of the night,
With every step, a tale unfolds,
Of ancient secrets, fiercely bold.

On icy winds, echoes call,
A symphony beneath the thrall,
Of sparkling realms, both fierce and grand,
A celestial gauntlet, quietly planned.

With heartbeats quickened, spirits sway,
In the cold embrace where shadows play,
Each moment a dance, a fleeting glance,
In the night's enchanting trance.

Twilight's Icy Serenade

As twilight's brush paints the sky,
Soft whispers of winter sigh,
Frosty lights in the fading glow,
Beneath the snow, dreams still flow.

A serenade of silvery chimes,
Echoing gentle, timeless rhymes,
Each note a snowflake's tender kiss,
In the quiet, frozen bliss.

Branches adorned with diamond tears,
Sway gently, calming all our fears,
The chill wraps close, a sweet embrace,
As night descends on this peaceful space.

Murmurs of twilight, soft and low,
Guide us where the cold winds blow,
With every breath, our spirits blend,
In this icy sheen, where dreams transcend.

In twilight's arms, let us remain,
In serene beauty, free from pain,
For in this moment, worlds collide,
In twilight's icy serenade, we bide.

The Quietude of Wintry Paths

In the hush where the snowflakes rest,
Whispers weave through the frozen vest,
Footprints mark the tranquil ground,
In the quiet, peace is found.

Gentle winds carry secrets old,
Through the branches, icy and bold,
Each step a story, soft and slow,
On wintry paths where shadows glow.

Frozen streams, a mirrored glass,
Reflect the beauty of seasons past,
In quietude, spirits roam,
Finding warmth in nature's home.

Moonlit beams dance on fields so wide,
A tapestry where dreams abide,
In the stillness, hearts unite,
In the beauty of the night.

Let us wander, hearts aglow,
Through fields of white where soft winds blow,
In quietude, we find our way,
On wintry paths, we wish to stay.

Hushed Footfalls on Frozen Streams

Upon the banks of crystal streams,
Footfalls whisper, lost in dreams,
Each crack and creak beneath our weight,
A song of ice, both crisp and great.

Beneath the stars, reflections play,
In the stillness, night turns gray,
As shadows blend with glimmering light,
To guide us through the heart of night.

Gentle breezes weave through trees,
Murmuring softly like the seas,
In frozen moments, we find grace,
As we trace the winter's face.

The world hushed under a blanket white,
Every breath a frosty bite,
In each footfall, the silence speaks,
In frozen joy, our spirit peaks.

Through winding paths where dreams align,
We navigate the stars that shine,
For in this dance on frozen streams,
We find the solace of our dreams.

Shadows on Shimmering Ice

Beneath the pale winter sky,
Shadows glide softly by.
Reflecting all that they see,
In a world of frozen glee.

Moonlight kisses the frozen ground,
Echoes of silence all around.
Whispers of winter take flight,
Painting the darkness with light.

Figures dance in the crystal night,
Casting spells, pure delight.
In the stillness they embrace,
All the charm of this space.

With the stars twinkling high,
The chilling breeze sighs.
In a moment made divine,
Every shadow intertwines.

As dawn breaks with gentle grace,
Fading from this magical place.
But the whispers still remain,
In the heart, a sweet refrain.

The Silent Dance of Winter

Snowflakes descend from the sky,
In a frosty ballet, they fly.
Silent whispers in the chill,
Nature pauses, time stands still.

Trees adorned in crystal lace,
Each branch holds a sacred space.
Beneath the moon's soft glow,
Winter's dance begins to flow.

Footprints trace a fleeting path,
In the quiet, feel the wrath.
But in the stillness, find your peace,
A moment where worries cease.

Stars sprinkle the endless night,
Guiding dreams in silver light.
With every breath, the cold air sings,
Of winter's love and what it brings.

As dawn unfolds with a sigh,
The silent dance waves goodbye.
Yet the memories linger on,
In the heart, where magic's drawn.

Beneath the Frosted Veil

Underneath a frosted veil,
Nature whispers a tender tale.
Of frozen lakes and silent trees,
Captured moments in the breeze.

The world sparkles, pure and bright,
In the holy hush of night.
Softly, snowflakes drift and fall,
Enveloping the earth in thrall.

Quiet footsteps mark the snow,
In a realm where dreamers go.
Whispers twirl like drifting leaves,
In the magic that winter weaves.

Branches heavy with glistening white,
A wondrous scene, pure delight.
Beneath the frost, life holds sway,
Resting till the warm spring day.

With every breath, the cold air hums,
In the quiet, a promise comes.
Beneath the veil, the world is whole,
In the heart, winter's soul.

Ethereal Journeys in White

Gentle whispers on the breeze,
A tapestry woven with ease.
In the hush of winter's night,
Ethereal journeys take flight.

Clouds like dreams float above,
Wrapping the world in a glove.
With each flake, a story unfolds,
Of warmth that the cold cannot hold.

Into the quiet, spirits glide,
Through frosted paths, side by side.
In a realm where magic thrives,
Winter's calm, where hope survives.

The moon beams down with a smile,
Illuminating the frosty mile.
In the stillness, hearts align,
Embracing peace, a love divine.

As dawn awakens from her sleep,
The world breathes in, taking deep.
Ethereal journeys softly end,
But winter's beauty will transcend.

Elfin Mists on the Twilight Walk

In twilight's glow where whispers play,
Elfin mists in soft array,
They dance along the forest floor,
Enchanting dreams forevermore.

A gentle breeze through branches weaves,
Tickling leaves with silver sleeves,
The nightingale sings sweet and low,
Underneath the stars' soft glow.

Glimmers of light adorn the trees,
Woven ties of twilight's breeze,
Where shadows meet the evening's peace,
And all the world's loud worries cease.

Footsteps echo on the path,
Guided home by nature's math,
Here, magic breathes in every sigh,
Beneath the ever-watchful sky.

Elfin mists, a shroud divine,
Where dreams and twilight gently intertwine,
A moment caught, forever bright,
In the soft embrace of fading light.

Shadows Beneath the Frosted Canopy

Underneath the frosted trees,
Shadows dance in winter's freeze,
Branches creak with each soft sigh,
Nature murmurs gently by.

Snowflakes drift like whispered dreams,
Cascading down in silver streams,
The world wrapped in a crystal sheet,
Where earth and sky delight to meet.

Frozen whispers fill the air,
Secrets only held with care,
The forest breathes a chilling song,
Echoing where we belong.

In twilight's arms, the shadows play,
Softened by the end of day,
While moonlight dances, pale and bright,
Beneath the canopy of night.

Every step upon the snow,
Leaves a tale of where we go,
Engulfed in beauty, still and bold,
Beneath the frosted leaves of old.

Echoes of Laughter on a Silvered Path

On a path where laughter reigns,
Echoes dance like gentle rains,
Silvered light reflects the joy,
Of every girl and every boy.

Windchimes of giggles in the air,
Memories twirl without a care,
Each moment glimmers like a star,
For happiness is never far.

Footprints trace the tales of old,
Stories waiting to be told,
In the hush, strands of delight,
Twine together, day to night.

Upon this silvered, winding way,
Laughter echoes, come what may,
A symphony of joy and peace,
Where every heart can find release.

Here, in the dance of time and space,
We find a kindred, warm embrace,
On a path where laughter flows,
The spirit of joy forever glows.

A Trail of Dreams Laced with Ice

A trail of dreams through frosty haze,
Whispers drift in winter's gaze,
Crystal shards beneath our feet,
As hope and wonder softly meet.

Beneath the stars that shimmer bright,
Each step leads us into the night,
A frozen realm where visions bloom,
In the quiet, we find our room.

The air is chilled, yet hearts ignite,
With dreams that warm the coldest night,
Each breath a mist, a promise clear,
Laced with ice, yet drawing near.

Through twilight paths, we wander free,
With every hope, a destiny,
As laughter rings through frosty air,
A trail of dreams, beyond compare.

A journey shared, where spirits fly,
In whispered secrets of the sky,
Together we unveil our fate,
On this sweet trail, we celebrate.

Milton Keynes UK
Ingram Content Group UK Ltd.
UKHW021400081224
452111UK00007B/108